Robin Hood

A Musical Celebration

David Wood
and
Dave and Toni Arthur

Samuel French – London
New York – Sydney – Toronto – Hollywood

ROBIN HOOD

ROBIN HOOD was first produced at the Nottingham Playhouse on 29th May 1981, by the Nottingham Playhouse Company, with the following cast of characters:

Jan, a milkmaid, dressed all in white; plays **"Maid Marian"** in the Robin Hood playlets   Jan Shand

Dorcas, a milkmaid at the beer bower; plays **"Pretty Maid"** (**"Allen-a-Dale"**'s bride)   Dorcas Jones

Tessa, a serving girl at the beer bower; plays **"Sheriff of Nottingham's Wife"**; **"Wedding Attendant"**   Tessa Wojtczak

Elizabeth, the ale wife, an older, buxom hostess of the beer bower; plays **"Abbess"**   Elizabeth Sinclair

Dikran, morris dancer 1, who plays **"Will Scarlet"**; **"Wedding Attendant"**   Dikran Tulaine

George, morris dancer 2, who plays **"Allen-a-Dale"**   George Winter

Philip, morris dancer 3, who plays **"Butcher"**; **"Single-stick Dueller"**; **"Monk"**; **"Old Knight"**   Philip Childs

Alan, morris dancer 4, who plays **"Sheriff of Nottingham"**; **"Single-stick Dueller"**; **"Monk"**   Alan Barker

Ross, morris dancer 5, who plays **"Tradesman"**; **"Wrestler"**; **"Sir Guy of Gisborne"**   Ross Davidson

John, morris dancer 6, who plays **"Tradesman"**; **"Wrestler"**; **"Bishop"**   John Rankin

Peter, the Jack-in-the-Green, who plays **"Robin Hood"**   Peter Woodward

Benedick, the Hobby-horse Rider (wearing hobby horse around him, held up by braces), who plays **"Little John"**   Benedick Blythe

Robin, the Fool (with traditional
    bladder), a tumbler, who remains
    as the **Fool**, organizer of the revels
    throughout   Robin Wright
Michael, the Comic Morris Friar, a
    traditional attendant of the
    morris, with funny nose, who
    plays **"Friar Tuck"**   Michael Remick
Thomas, a serving boy, who plays
    "Much" the miller's son   Thomas Hain

Directed by Crispin Thomas
Musical direction by David Epps
Choreography by Lynn Britt
Designed by Hugh Durrant
Fights arranged by Peter Woodward

The play was subsequently performed by the Young Vic
Company at the Young Vic. The first performance was
on 9th December, 1982, with the following cast:

John Boswall	Jeffery Kissoon
Nina Botting	Clive Mantle
Amanda Boxer	Robert Morgan
Patch Connolly	Emma Rogers
Liz Crowther	Michael Simkins
Ross Davidson	Howard Southern
David Dodimead	Ian Taylor
Andrew Hawkins	Frank Vincent

The play was directed by David Toguri
Setting by Bernard Culshaw
Costumes designed by John Fraser
Lighting designed by Andy Phillips
Fights arranged by Ian McKay
Music arranged and directed by Peter Fincham

STORIES ACTED OUT DURING THE MAY GAMES

ACT I
Robin Hood and Friar Tuck
Robin Hood and Little John
Robin Hood and the Butcher

ACT II
Robin Hood and Sir Guy of Gisborne
Robin Hood and the Bishop
Robin Hood and Allen-a-Dale

MUSICAL NUMBERS

ACT I

1   I've Been A-Rambling
1a   Who's the Jack?
2   Bring Us In Good Ale
3   Circle Dance
4   Allen-a-Dale's Song
5   Join Us In Our Games
6   Summer Sun
7   Allen-a-Dale's Link Song
8   Stick Dance
9   Wild Flowers
10   Allen-a-Dale's Link Song
11   Horn Dance
12   Take the Scorn
12a   Hal-an-tow

ACT II

13   Hal-an-tow (Reprise)
14   Allen-a-Dale's Link Song
15   Sword Dance
16   This Ae Night
16a   O Heavenly Father
17   Dance, Dance
18   Before the Maid Weds
19   Wedding Hymn
20   Dance, Dance (Reprise)
21   Circle Dance (Reprise)

The music for this play is on hire from Samuel French Ltd

INTRODUCTION

Not so long ago it was traditional in England for May Day to be celebrated with organized May Games. These were organized at local or municipal level and comprised a variety of pastimes, ranging from processional and round *dances*, competitive *sports*, and *pageants*, as well as *plays*. May Day was a public holiday, on which to celebrate the rebirth of the year. It was inevitable that such celebrations should take on the element of ritual and superstition; after all, the livelihood of the majority of the participants would depend on the success of the coming harvest, and everybody would be hoping for good luck.

The May Games took place in an open space, such as a village green, where a maypole would be erected, with fresh greenery from the woods as decoration. This area would be looked upon as hallowed ground with "magical" properties. To satisfy the physical needs of the villagers a beer bower would be erected with ale often supplied by the local corporation.

The May celebrations started on magical May Eve, when folk went into the woods to gather the greenery to decorate the village. These excursions frequently developed into horseplay or drunken orgies, setting the tone of the following May Day activities.

The folk hero, Robin Hood, played a dominant role in the May Games. Stories about him were often played out between the morris dancing and other entertainments. These activities continued throughout the day, until the culmination of the Games, when "Robin Hood" would be ritualistically married to "Maid Marian". This represented the marriage of the King and Queen of the May, and symbolized fertility, which would hopefully lead to a rich harvest.

The stories and characters of the Robin Hood legend are thought to have developed in no small measure from their May Games presentations. In the few remaining ballads of Robin Hood, there is very little mention of Maid Marian and Friar Tuck. It is thought that they may well have been absorbed into the Robin Hood legend from their participation in the May Games; the buffoon friar was an accepted attendant of the morris, along with the Hobby Horse and Jack-in-the-Green (covered in the greenery of Spring), and Marian was perhaps based on the Queen of the May, the local girl chosen to "marry" the Lord of the May in the ritualistic wedding.

This setting provides the framework for our play—a re-creation of the May Games. The fact that May Games village characters act roles in the Robin Hood plays, enables the stories to be narrated and acted out in a spirited, stylized, even exaggerated manner, rather than attempting a naturalistic recreation of Sherwood Forest. In other words, the style and atmosphere of the Robin Hood playlets should be a complete contrast to the enactments of the May Games. The different styles of acting could well be enhanced by different styles of lighting.

Traditionally the dominant colours of summer were *green and white*; in this play, whoever plays **Robin Hood**, in other words whichever actor is playing the villager who plays **Robin Hood**, will be dressed in a basic green; the actress playing the local milkmaid, who will play **Maid Marian**, and eventually "marry" **Robin Hood**, will be dressed in all white.

All the other characters should be dressed as villagers, perhaps depicting various crafts and trades. The period setting of the play is at the director's discretion, although we feel that the early nineteenth century is probably about right. The basic villagers' costumes should be the everyday clothes of whichever period is selected, except those of the morris dancers—they should be dressed in the decorative ribboned costumes usually associated with them.

In the original production, financial restrictions meant that the cast could not exceed fourteen in number. This meant that the morris dancers had to also play parts in the Robin Hood plays. We would like to make it clear, however, that we envisage many productions of the play in which large numbers of local people take part, not just the local dramatic society! This would mean that the morris dancers would be the real local morris dancers, who would not be asked to do more than dance as indicated. The involvement of the local community could further be extended in terms of folk serving drinks from the beer bower, dressed appropriately. Or a large number of extras could represent other villagers, who play no part in the Robin Hood plays; a complete Mayor and Corporation could be seated in places of honour, and the Mayor could himself declare the Games open. The local Women's Institute could perhaps provide food cooked to old-fashioned recipes, sold by "traders" wandering amongst the audience.

Children could well be used as villagers. They could join in the singing and dancing, as well as provide a useful extra dimension to the "audience". In the first production, it was decided to use a young local amateur actor to play **Much**, the miller's son; as a character in the play his presence was not essential, but as an extra number of the outlaw band, he provided an entertaining contrast in size.

It seems to us that the possibilities for the involvement of a community are endless. Nevertheless, it must be pointed out that the play can be produced, as in the original production, with a basic cast of fourteen talented people.

The "team-playing" required of the cast demands good singers, movers, actors, acrobats, and a clear range of "types", as found in any village. They will remain in their "basic" all the time, adding a cloak and/or hat to "become", say, a bishop or monk. It is suggested that each Robin Hood character has an "emblem", or identification factor, which is a prop or a piece of costume, put on before the commencement of a Robin Hood story, and taken off afterwards. This could be organized by the Fool. We hope that it will help add clarity, in the sense that the audience will be able to distinguish clearly between the May Games sections of the play and the Robin Hood playlets themselves.

Perhaps tents or trestle tables and benches and the beer bower itself can be used for quick changes; but these should, in the main, be done in full view of the audience, to increase the feeling of improvization—miming out the story "as it happens". Occasional moments will be found where the May Games character is rather uneasy in his Robin Hood role—for example, the **Friar**, who physically may not live up to the description of him; his slight embarrassment can be a source of amusement to his fellow May Games folk.

Because the actors are playing villagers, who then assume Robin Hood roles, we feel that for simplicity's sake, it is advisable for the villagers to be called by the actors' own names. Naturally this is not essential, but it may seem over-complex if an actor called Peter is playing a villager called "Charles" who is playing "Robin Hood" . . . It seems to us much better, as well as more fun for the actors, if Peter is called by his own name throughout the play, except when he is playing Robin Hood.

Audience participation may be encouraged, vocally—particularly in the sung refrains—and, if the staging permits—physically, in some of the dances. At all times, the audience should feel part of the community celebrating.

Needless to say, the play need not be performed in any particular space. Already performances have been seen in a promenade production, with the action taking place amongst the audience, as well as on a proscenium stage. We envisage open-air productions of the play, maybe even taking place on real village greens.

It should rarely be necessary for any actor to leave the acting area. Whenever somebody is not actively involved, he should remain on as audience.

The music probably needs to be played by two or three musicians resident on a band stand, augmented by a strolling musician playing fiddle, guitar or, if possible, tabor and pipe. Nearly all the cast should play percussion instruments to punctuate the narrative of the Robin Hood playlets, as well as keep up the rhythmic excitement of the May Games.

Where **Narrator** is mentioned in the script, it is suggested that the director choose an available character to narrate, or divide the narration between several members of the company.

The actor playing **Allen-a-Dale** should play a lute, or lute-shaped guitar if possible. Props should be simple—ideally existing paraphernalia of the May Games should be used to *suggest* settings and props of the Robin Hood stories. For example, a trestle table can become a bridge; morris dancers' staffs can become trees; the Hobby Horse can "play" the bishop's horse; decorative blue ribbons could be used to represent a stream.

It is *suggested* that above the action a large round screen with back projections could be used to suggest the moon and the sun (to indicate, by its position, the time of day), as well as project images relating to the action. For example, *antlers* or *longbow*.

*   *   *   *

Please see the back of this Acting Edition for an Appendix describing the various dances suggested.

David Wood and Dave and Toni Arthur

PROLOGUE*

This introduction to the play is optional. For the original production it was considered a good idea to set up the idea of the May Games of yesteryear, and at the same time to establish the atmosphere and background to the show

Although the prologue is written in such a way that each member of the cast has his or her own line, we believe that the prologue would work equally well spoken by one actor, or indeed by all the cast in unison

It is suggested that before the show starts, the cast are already mingling with the audience. As the House Lights begin to fade, the cast join hands, forming a circle in the centre of the playing area, and when the audience is hushed, the prologue is spoken

Ben Come back with us to yesteryear, to a time when we all lived closer to nature.

Tessa We had a sense of wonder then, and superstition and magic were real in our hearts.

Dickran We crossed our fingers. We carried salt in our pockets for good luck.

Jan From the cradle to the grave we performed our rituals to bring health and prosperity to crops and animals and men.

Philip Tonight is April the thirtieth, so we're off to the woods to gather green boughs, to decorate our village.

Alan For tomorrow's the first of May, the beginning of summer, new life, new hope, rebirth.

Ross It's a holiday. It's a day to celebrate. We'll have May Games on the green.

Robin We'll dance and sing, and drink, and display our skills.

John We'll tell you stories of bold Robin Hood, the Green Man, the Lord of the Wood.

George We'll choose our King and Queen of the May.

Dorcas And marry them under the maypole, the very symbol of life and fertility.

Elizabeth So let traditions and customs be remembered again.

Michael Please. Share them with us. Everyone.

---

*N.B. Paragraph 3 on page ii of this Acting Edition regarding photocopying and video-recording should be carefully read.

ACT I

An empty space

The Lights fade to Black-out. Echoing footsteps of a nightwatchman are heard. A church-clock bell chimes 2 o'clock

Voice 1 (*through the darkness*) Two of the clock, may the good lord keep . . .

A handbell rings

Voice 2 The goblins from you whilst you sleep.

The handbell rings. The church-clock bell chimes 3 o'clock. Shafts of moonlight slowly fade up

Voice 3 Three of the clock, and all's well.

The handbell rings

Voice 4 So says the man that rings the bell.

The handbell rings. The church-clock chimes 4 o'clock. The moonlight becomes brighter

Voice 5 Four of the clock, good-day to you.

The handbell rings

Voice 6 Maids go gather the magic dew.

The handbell rings

> *Three giggling maids—Dorcas, Tessa and Jan—enter excitedly. They mime gathering dew in their hands and washing their faces with it*

All   I wash my face in the morning dew,
                     For this is the First of May,
                     Wash in the dew and wishes come true,
                     For this is the First of May.
Jan   Oh make me pretty, make my skin
                     As white as driven snow,
Dorcas   Make me fair as any rose,
Tessa   Make my freckles go.

From her drawstring purse Jan produces "magic" ash-leaves and distributes them. General giggling and then serious concentration for the forthcoming "spell"

Dorcas   Magic ash-leaf in my glove,
                        Lead me to the one I love.

She closes her eyes and covers them with her hands, then wishes out loud

   George!

General giggles

Tessa   Magic ash-leaf on my palm,
                        Lead me to the one I'll charm.

She closes her eyes and wishes

   Dickran!

General giggles

Jan   Magic ash-leaf that I carry,
                        Lead me to the one I'll marry.

She closes her eyes, but makes her wish silently, not revealing whom she fancies

Dorcas Go on, Jan ...
Tessa Who do you see?
Jan (*as if in a dream*) Peter is the one for me!

The Lights fade as we hear a solo voice

   The three maids slip away

As the singing continues, the Lights fade up. Dawn is rising

   The solo singer (Dickran) enters, carrying a large May bough

Music 1: I've Been A-Rambling

Dickran   I've been a-rambling half the night
(*singing*)   And the best part of the day;
                        And now I'm returning home again
                        And I've brought you a branch of May.

Philip enters from the other side, carrying a large May bough—a leafy branch

Philip   Oh arise, arise, you pretty fair maid,
(*singing*)   And take your May-bush in;

The Lights continue to rise in the background

                        For if it is gone before tomorrow morn
                        You will say we have brought you none.

Dorcas and Jan and (possibly) children enter from another place, carrying decorated hoops—ribbons and greenery with May dolls suspended in the middle of hoops, which are about two feet in diameter

Dorcas ⎫	Good-morning ladies and gentlemen
Jan ⎬	It is the first of May
Children ⎭	We hope you'll view our garland
	It is so small and gay.

I love my little brother
And sister every day,
But I seem to love them better
In the merry month of May.

A drum beats. Instrumental chords

Enter a strolling musician (George), playing a lute or guitar, followed by a decorated cart pulled by Alan and Ross. The cart contains general decorations and greenery; also Peter, hidden inside a large Jack-in-the-Green garland. John pushes the cart

From the opposite side, enter the Comic Morris Friar (Michael), and the Fool (Robin) with his bladder on a stick, bopping the Friar and the audience on the head

From another entrance appears the Hobby Horse, danced by Benedick, attended by a Boy

All sing as they process to the Maypole area

All   Come you young men haste along
(*singing*)   With your music and your song
                 Take your lasses in your hand

Dikran and another Morris Dancer take Dorcas and Jan and dance a hey (such as a country-dancing figure of eight)

For 'tis that which spring commands;
Then to the maypole haste away

The Boy, the Fool and two others fetch the maypole and erect it in the centre of the space

For 'tis now a holiday.

Musical break as the cast dance or watch the maypole going up. Cheers. Then some start decorating the area with greenery from the cart. They make a "beer bower" (or refreshment "tent") and set out tables and benches

'Tis the choice time of the year
For the violets now appear;
Now the rose receives its birth
And pretty primroses deck the earth;
Then to the maypole haste away
For 'tis now a holiday.

The music continues as the Jack-in-the-Green garland in the cart begins to move mysteriously. It stands up, watched intently by the crowd. A green spotlight picks up the green mound, which starts to sway to the music

Dickran Look, the very garland dances.
Philip When was such a wonder seen?
Alan Hey! Let's look a little closer.

They discover Peter "inside" the garland

Ross There's a Jack within the Green!

Dickran, Philip, Alan and Ross get the Jack-in-the-Green off the cart. The rest of the crowd take up a chant, starting quietly and building up to an intense climax. During the chant, they join hands around the Jack-in-the-Green and circle clockwise round it, gradually speeding up

Music 1(a): Who's the Jack?

All	Who's the Jack?
(*chanting*)	Who's the Jack?
	Who's the Jack-in-the-Green?
	Bring him out!
	Bring him out!
(*With a shout*)	It's time for him to be *seen*.

The chant is repeated several times as required. Finally, all stop and stretch towards the Jack-in-the-Green. Drums echo the tension. The cast freeze. Philip and Alan approach the Jack-in-the-Green in ritualistic manner, almost like priests, and ceremonially remove the garland. Peter steps out with arms outstretched to the crowd. Chord. The crowd is still frozen as Jan moves forward to peer at the revealed figure. Lights pick up Peter and Jan

Jan It's Peter.

Jan's cry breaks the spell. The cast crowd round Peter, and lead him to the maypole

All Welcome, Peter . . . etc.

The Comic Friar (Michael) steps forward, as Peter's garland "cloak" is removed

Comic Friar   Jack-in-the-Green is the Lord of the May;
                            To the top of the Maypole hoist him away.

Drums beat as Dickran, Philip, Alan and Ross hoist the garland to the top of the maypole, signalling the start of the May Games. The lighting begins to increase

                            The games begin, the Maypole's crowned,
                            And Peter's the King till the sun goes down.

Cheers from the crowd. Peter walks to the front, his arms raised. He is lit dramatically from above, below and behind, by shafts of light

Peter   If I am to be the King of the day
                            Then drinks on me—there's nothing to pay.

    All cheer

Peter turns upstage, arm outstretched. Music starts—a drumbeat intro to "Bring Us In Good Ale"

Music 2: Bring Us In Good Ale

(*singing*)   Bring us in good ale oh, bring us in good ale
All   For our blessed lady's sake, bring us in good ale.

The Lighting becomes more general, as from the beer bower, Tessa and Elizabeth bring in trays of ale to general cheers. Everyone collects a drink. Then the company splits into two halves

Group 1   Bring us in no bacon that is very fat;
Group 2   Bring us in good ale and give us enough of that.

Both groups repeat the first verse as a round

All   Bring us in good ale oh, bring us in good ale
               Bring us in good ale oh, bring us in good ale
               For our blessed lady's sake
               Bring us in good ale.

General merriment during the singing develops into a Circle Dance around the maypole, involving all except George

Music 3: Circle Dance

As the dance finishes, everyone sits down for a rest. George is revealed, strumming his lute/guitar

Comic Friar Come on, George, give us a song!

The others call their approval as George comes forward

George Which one do you want to hear?
Jan Give us the one about Robin Hood.

Cheers of agreement

George All right. Who's going to play Robin?
Philip Peter, of course. He's our King of the May!

Cheers as Peter steps forward

George What about Maid Marian?

The girls' hands shoot up

   (*Choosing*) Jan.

Cheers. George starts playing the introduction. The Lighting changes

Music 4: Allen-a-Dale's Song

George's lines could be shared with other villagers if required

George (*singing*)   There were stories told in the days of old,

Of men of might and main;
But the greatest man was a Nottingham lamb
And Robin was his name.
Robin, Robin,
And he took his name from the bird in the wood,
And they called him Robin Hood.

There's some would make him a fine lord's son,
A belted earl at least,
But the silver spoon that he used at noon,
He stole from a canting priest.

He begins to take in the whole audience, encouraging them to join in the chorus

All   Robin, Robin,
And he took his name from the bird in the wood,
And they called him Robin Hood.

As the story progresses, the company mime out the story as required, perhaps in silhouette against a sheet held up by the others, or wearing masks. In the original production, puppets on long poles were carried by the actors, following the action in the song. Peter plays "Robin Hood"

George   His mother she came from a castle fine
But a yeoman's love she found,
And she left her home with her love to roam
Through Sherwood the seasons round.

All   Robin, Robin
And he took his name from the bird in the wood,
And they called him Robin Hood.

George   Robin was born on a bracken couch,
Down on the forest floor,
His mother she wept as the baby slept,
For the home she'd see no more.

All   Robin, Robin,
And she took his name from the bird in the wood,
And she called him Robin Hood.

George   Robin he grew to a fine young man,
Well-skilled with staff and bow,
And far and near he'd hunt the deer,
That through the woods did go.

All   Robin, Robin,
And he took his name from the bird in the wood,
And they called him Robin Hood.

George   News has reached the Sheriff's ears
And it's whispered door to door
That young Robin Hood, who lives in the wood
Robs the rich to feed the poor.

All   Robin, Robin,
And they took his name from the bird in the wood,
And they called him Robin Hood.

"Robin Hood" steps forward, putting on a waistcoat or other "identification"

"Robin Hood" For the hunting of the king's royal deer,
An outlaw I became,
And I made a vow that I ne'er would bow,
And the rich would fear my name.
All Robin, Robin,
"Robin Hood" And I took my name from the bird in the wood,
And they call me Robin Hood.

I gathered the finest band of men,
That walked on English ground,
With the grey goose feather and the silken string
No better could be found.

The music continues as "Robin Hood" selects his "outlaws"—from the villagers. They react flattered or embarrassed

There was er ... (*choosing his "cast"*) fair Maid
Marian and Little John
They came to join the fun
And Allen and Will in scarlet still
And Much the miller's son.

They came to the wood from ev'ry shire
And they ate the doe and buck;
And the hungriest man in the outlaw band
Was the jovial Friar Tuck.

The Comic Friar is pushed forward to play "Friar Tuck" and conducts the final chorus. It is suggested that, if he is wearing a comic nose, he should remove this to signify the change of character

All Robin, Robin,
And he took his name from the bird in the wood
And we called him Robin Hood.

The Comic Friar is left c, *as the lighting changes back to the May Games lighting*

Philip How come a friar became an outlaw?
Dorcas Yes. Hardly the job for a holy man.
Ross Maybe he wasn't wholly holy! Get it? Wholly holy!

Laughter

Dickran No! Friar Tuck joined Robin Hood's band because ... (*He has an idea*) We'll show you.

He indicates the Comic Friar, who is about to put his nose back on

Won't we?
Comic Friar Will we?
Dickran We will.
Comic Friar (*reluctantly; he is nervous of playacting*) Oh.

Dickran (*announcing*) The story of Robin Hood and the Friar.

The villagers applaud, and prepare to hear and act out the story, which introduces the idea of the villagers playing Robin Hood roles

The May Games Comic Friar has to enact the role of "Friar Tuck"—and as the story begins with its exaggerated picture of "Friar Tuck", the May Games Comic Friar should find it difficult to live up to the description. Therefore the story itself only really gets under way once the transition of the embarrassed May Games Comic Friar into his "Friar Tuck" role has been completed. Naturally the villagers, as audience, find their colleague's discomfort funny

Drumbeats punctuate the action, as Dikran begins to tell the story. The lighting changes

Dickran Friar Tuck was the fattest of friars.

"Friar Tuck" puffs himself up, or the villagers could stuff cushions up his costume

   The merriest of friars.
"Friar Tuck" Ho, ho, ho!
Dickran And the holiest of friars.

"Friar Tuck" prays

   In fact it is said Friar Tuck was holier than his socks. And strong. He was so strong he could pick up any man and carry him like a babe in his arms.

Benedick offers himself to be carried—"Friar Tuck" looks at the huge man, decides against it, and picks up the Boy. Cheers. Laughter

   He could eat any man under the table.

"Friar Tuck" takes the Boy under a table and mimes biting him

   What are you doing?

"Friar Tuck" Eating a man under the table.

Laughter

Dickran And when it came to drinking . . . he could drink more ale in less time than any man in Nottingham.

Drums as Tessa brings out, say, four tankards of beer (trick glasses). "Friar Tuck" looks worried, but, encouraged by the villagers, joins in the spirit of things—downing all four pints! Cheers from the crowd after each glass is downed

   What's more the drink had no effect on him whatsoever.

"Friar Tuck" collapses in the arms of two villagers

   His eating and drinking habits got him expelled from his abbey.

The villagers throw him down

Villagers Out!

Dickran As a penance he used to carry travellers over a stream where the bridge was broken.

The company create the stream using ropes or ribbons and rippling them. We now go into the story proper

One morning he was sitting by the stream deep in meditation . . .

"Friar Tuck" snores

When he was interrupted by a voice from the opposite bank.

Enter "Robin Hood", carrying a bag, which he puts down on the ground

"Robin Hood" Hey! Fat Friar.
"Friar Tuck" (*waking with a start*) Mm? What?
"Robin Hood" Are you the fat friar that ferries?
"Friar Tuck" For my sins, I am.
"Robin Hood" Good. Carry me across, Friar.
"Friar Tuck" Certainly, my son. If you come over here, I'll carry you across.
"Robin Hood" Right. (*He approaches the water*) Hey. Wait a minute. You take me for a mug? If I come over to you, I'll have to cross the stream and get wet. Not only that, if I come over to your side and then you carry me across, I'll end up back on this side instead of that side.
"Friar Tuck" Life is full of little problems, my son.
"Robin Hood" I want to get to that side, not this side, and I don't want to get wet. You'll have to come and collect me, fatty Friar.
"Friar Tuck" Cheek. You can stay there.
"Robin Hood" Very well. I'll eat my pie instead.
"Friar Tuck" (*interested*) Pie. Did you say pie?
"Robin Hood" Venison. I'd offer you some, if you were over this side.
"Friar Tuck" Venison you say?
"Robin Hood" Best venison pie, yes.
"Friar Tuck" (*tempted*) I'm coming over.

Music. "Friar Tuck" wades over the stream. Ooohs and Aaahs in the cold water. He arrives

"Robin Hood" Welcome, fat Friar. (*He prepares to jump on "Friar Tuck's" back*)
"Friar Tuck" You mentioned some pie, my son . . .
"Robin Hood" Of course. You can have half of it. *Over there.*
"Friar Tuck" Where?
"Robin Hood" There.

The "Over there." "Where?" "Over there!" becomes a catch phrase, taken up and joined in by the Company whenever it crops up in the story

"Friar Tuck" Where?
All There.
"Robin Hood" Carry me across the stream and I'll give you the pie.
"Friar Tuck" (*greed winning the day*) Amen, my son, you win.

Music. "Friar Tuck" carries "Robin Hood" over on his back. He puffs and pants under the strain

"Robin Hood" Thank you, Friar. God be with you. (*He starts to go*)
"Friar Tuck" Wait. The er . . . the pie.
"Robin Hood" Of course. I'm sorry. (*He feels for his bag*) Oh no. I've left it over there. (*He points to his bag on the other bank*)
"Friar Tuck" Where?
All There.
"Robin Hood" You'll have to carry me back.
"Friar Tuck" Oh no, you can get it yourself.
"Robin Hood" I'm not really very hungry.
"Friar Tuck" I am.
"Robin Hood" Carry me back, then.
"Friar Tuck" Amen, my son, you win.

"Robin Hood" starts to mount

Wait. What happens when I carry you across?
"Robin Hood" I give you the pie.
"Friar Tuck" Then what?
"Robin Hood" You carry me back across.
"Friar Tuck" No, no, no. I tell you what. I'll get on your back, you take me back, you give me the pie, you get on my back and I bring you back here.
"Robin Hood" Fair enough.

Music. With difficulty "Robin Hood" carries "Friar Tuck" across. "Robin Hood" finds the pie

Thank you, fat Friar, here's your pie.

"Friar Tuck" starts stuffing his face

Come on.
"Friar Tuck" What?
"Robin Hood" You've got to carry me. Over there.
"Friar Tuck" Where?
All There.
"Friar Tuck" Sorry, my son. I never let work interfere with food.
"Robin Hood" But you agreed.
"Friar Tuck" Sorry.
"Robin Hood" I'll make you sorry—(*he draws his sword*)—I want to cross the stream. Now.
"Friar Tuck" (*reacting to the sword*) Amen, my son, you win.

Music. "Friar Tuck" carries "Robin Hood" into the "water". Then drops him halfway. "Friar Tuck" returns to the bank. "Robin Hood" splashes around in the "water"

(*Laughing*) That'll teach you.

"Robin Hood" struggles out of the "water"

"Robin Hood" You fiendish Friar. I'll teach *you*. Come on. I challenge you.

"Robin Hood's" sword is drawn. "Friar Tuck" leaps up eagerly

"Friar Tuck" A fight, a fight. Splendid.

Music. Then fight—sword and bucklers. The company cheers them on. "Friar Tuck" is much stronger than "Robin Hood" thought. Eventually "Robin Hood" is helpless on the ground

"Robin Hood" (*breathless*) A favour. Grant me a favour!
"Friar Tuck" Very well.

"Robin Hood" blows his horn. Music as some villagers stop being spectators and become "Outlaws"; they rush in, surround "Friar Tuck" and drag him off "Robin Hood"

"Robin Hood" My men!
"Friar Tuck" A favour! Grant me a favour.
"Robin Hood" Very well.

"Friar Tuck" makes a strange calling noise. Other villagers stop being spectators, put on dog masks, and rush on barking. They quickly overpower the "Outlaws", and stand over them, panting

"Friar Tuck" My dogs!

"Robin Hood" laughs

"Robin Hood" A truce! A truce! Good Friar, I like you. You're a man of spirit.
"Friar Tuck" I like you too. My two favourite activities are food and fighting, and you've given me both. What is your name, my son?
"Robin Hood" Men call me Robin Hood.
"Friar Tuck" You are Robin Hood?
"Robin Hood" Yes. And I invite you to become our chaplain and help us further God's work against tyranny and oppression.

Cheers

"Friar Tuck" I accept.

Cheers

"Robin Hood" We shall call you—Friar Tuck! (*Giving him the pie*) Follow us—the feast is about to start.
"Friar Tuck" Feast! What are we celebrating?
"Robin Hood" I'll give you the toast ... (*He steps forward formally*)

> To life in the greenwood
> To flowers and trees
> The sun and the rain
> The birds and the bees
> To justice, to right
> Let us joyfully sing
> To goodness and truth
> To God and our King!

All   To God and our King!

Cheers

"Friar Tuck" A moment my son.

"Friar Tuck" steps forward, and starts his prayer. The others put their hands together solemnly

> May the Lord above
> Send down a dove
> To bring us all his benison
> And on my knee
> My fervent plea
> Is——(*Breaking the atmosphere*)
> Where d'you keep your venison?

Laughter

The lighting fades up to bright sunlight. We are back at the May Games. The villagers congratulate those who acted in the story. Peter removes his "Robin Hood" identification. "Friar Tuck" replaces his comic nose to become once more the Comic Friar. It is important at this stage that the village May Games atmosphere is re-established

Music 5: Join Us In Our Games

A drumbeat, perhaps played by the Fool, leads the villagers into a song. During it, food and drink are brought on, and the audience are invited to celebrate. Perhaps villagers can offer some of the audience refreshments. During the song, Benedick is seen to drink more than the others

All (*singing*)   Join us in our games
> Join us in our games
> There's only one thing that we pray—
> Let love and friendship rule this day,
> And grant us all a joyful May
> So join us in our games.

> Join us in our games
> Join us in our games
> There's songs to sing and plays to play
> To brighten up this holiday,
> So take your partners while you may
> And join us in our games.

> Join us in our games
> Join us in our games
> There's pies and pudding, quince and quail
> And maids and young men should not fail
> To quaff a quart of Nottingham ale
> And join us in our games.

Join us in our games
Join us in our games
Our dances are well tried and true
We've dances old and dances new
We've come today to dance for you
So join us in our games.

Music continues, as the Morris Dancers assemble, having put bells round their knees. They perform a celebratory handkerchief dance

There's only one thing that we pray
Let love and friendship rule this day,
And grant us all a joyful May
So join us in our games.

At the end of the song and dance, applause and cameraderie. Men kiss the women. Relaxation. Lying in the sun

Jan, on her own, sings reflectively towards Peter

Music 6: Summer Sun

Jan   Summer sun shining down
                         Shining down from above,
                         Look at me, shine on me
                         I'm a young girl in love.
                         Make me queen for today
                         Let me welcome the May
                         In the arms, in the arms,
                         In the arms of my rambling Robin.

                         I love him can't you see
                         Won't you please let it be,
                         Let the magic of ash leaf
                         And sun work for me.
                         If the Jack-in-the-Green
                         Lets me be his May Queen
                         Then I'll dance, then I'll dance,
                         Then I'll dance for my rambling Robin.

She dances amongst the villagers—favouring Peter

                         Summer sun shining down
                         Shining down from above
                         Look at me, shine on me,
                         I'm a young girl in love.
                         Make me queen for today
                         Let me welcome the May
                         In the arms, in the arms,
                         In the arms of my rambling Robin
All Girls   In the arms, in the arms,
                         In the arms of my rambling Robin.

Benedick spies Jan. He is fairly drunk, in a happy rather than unpleasant way. He grabs Jan from behind and tries to kiss her

Jan Come on, Benedick, sit down—before you fall down.
Benedick Ah, it's Jan, the fair milkmaid. Give us a kiss.
Jan You're drunk.
Benedick With love, fair Jan. Drunk with love. Give us a kiss.
Jan Leave off, Benedick, you've had too much.
Benedick I could never have too much of you. I could drink your milk till the cows come home.

Onlookers laugh. Benedick picks Jan up

Jan (*giggly rather than cross*) Put me down, you great bear. I can't be yours. The ash leaf said I was Peter's for today.
Benedick Ash leaf? Ash leaf? What does an ash leaf know about true love? Come on, give us a kiss.

She escapes him and runs away. He chases her in and out of the others. Finally, Peter sticks out his foot. Benedick trips over it and falls headlong

What did you do that for, Peter? I almost caught her then.
Peter Caught her? Caught her? You're too slow to catch a cold!
Benedick Too slow am I? I'm quick enough to give you a headache.
Peter Come on then, prove it!

They start fighting

Elizabeth Hey. Come on. It's May Day.
Michael Break it up!
George No! Stay there.

Suddenly the action freezes, and the lighting changes, as George comes forward, playing his lute/guitar. He sings us into the story of "Robin Hood and Little John"

Music 7: Allen-a-Dale's Link Song

(*Singing*)   I'll tell you a story of bold Robin Hood

Peter becomes "Robin Hood" (putting on his identification factor)

And a man who was strong as an ox;

Benedick becomes "Little John" (putting on his identification factor)

Though little by name
He was massive of frame
And he stood seven foot in his socks.
They happened to meet on a long narrow
    bridge . . .

"Robin Hood" and "Little John" look round. They see a trestle table and, deciding to use it as the bridge in the story, leap up on to it. A Narrator picks up the story, which is now acted out before the rest of the company, who join in

as required, or simply watch the play. The Narrator throws a quarterstaff each to "Robin Hood" and "Little John"

Narrator	They happened to meet on a long narrow bridge
	Where the river was deep and fast flowing.
	Smiled Robin—
"Robin Hood" (*speaking*)	Good day!
Narrator	The giant said,
"Little John" (*speaking*)	Hey,
	Just where do you think you are going?
"Robin Hood"	I want to cross over.
"Little John"	And so do I;
	And I sense that you're blocking my route.
"Robin Hood"	Now you let me pass
	Or I swear your fat ass
	Will sense the tip of my boot!
"Little John"	Ha ha, ho ho ho, ha ha, ho ho ho,
Narrator	The giant defiantly laughed.
"Little John"	You maggot, you flea,
	You dare challenge me?
	Are you mad or incredibly daft?
"Robin Hood"	Will you budge?
Narrator	asked Robin,
"Little John"	Like hell I will!
	You tadpole?
"Robin Hood"	You beanpole! You lout!
Narrator	And raising his staff hit
	This hardbitten half-wit
	A walloping well-aimed clout.
	The giant gave Robin a crack on the crown
	That caused the blood to run.
"Little John"	Am I playing too rough?
	Have you had enough?
Narrator	Replied Robin,
"Robin Hood"	I've hardly begun!

A stylized quarterstaff fight sequence, accompanied by drums and cheering and booing from rival supporters. The fight reaches a crescendo. Deadlock. Lighting changes as the fight becomes a stylized slow-motion fight, maybe in strobe lighting, which continues silently as the narration resumes

Narrator	Bang, bang, the quarterstaffs rang
	As hour after hour they did pummel and pound;
	Smashing and straining,
	Bashing and braining,
	But neither was willing to give any ground.
	The giant was getting as good as he gave
	As Robin clung on and gritted his teeth.

But with one final blow
He laid Robin low
And tumbled him into the water beneath.

"Robin Hood" falls off the "bridge" and thrashes around in the "water".
Cheers and boos from the rival supporters. Lighting returns to normal

	He thrashed and he splashed.
"Little John"	That'll teach you, my friend
	You were wrong to take me for a mug.
	Now who's won the day? What have you got to say?
Narrator	And Robin replied,
"Robin Hood"	Glug, glug, glug.

I have to admit, sir, you fought fair and square,
And in truth you're the winner hands down.
If I don't speak at length
Of your courage and strength
It's because I am starting to drown.

"Robin Hood" struggles, then manages to blow his horn. At this moment some
of the villagers become "Robin Hood's men" and rush in. They stand watching
"Robin Hood" in the "water"

"Will Scarlett"	What on earth's going on?
Narrator	Will Scarlett exclaimed.
"Will Scarlett"	Our master is soaked to the skin.
"Robin Hood"	Look don't hang about
	Come on, pull me out!
	Don't wager on how I fell in!

They help him out

Narrator	When they heard how it happened, the outlaws went wild ...

They grab "Little John"

"Outlaws"	This villain shall not go scot-free.
	Let's duck him likewise!
Narrator	But Robin Hood cries
"Robin Hood"	He's Robin Hood's friend, let him be.

They drop "Little John"

"Little John"	Robin Hood? Robin Hood? Are you Robin Hood?
Narrator	The stranger grabbed hold of his hand.
"Little John"	I was coming to meet you
	To greet you not beat you
	I want to be one of your band.

The "Outlaws" cheer. "Robin Hood" welcomes him, shaking his hand and
introducing him to the others. George comes forward

Music 7a

George (*singing*)	Robin welcomed the giant, John Little by name
"Robin Hood"	
(*speaking*)	You're one of my men from now on
George	And because of his size
	It was no great surprise—
	John Little became
All (*with a shout*)	Little John!

Fanfare. Applause. "Robin Hood" and "Little John" bow. The lighting fades back up to the May Games state. "Robin Hood" and "Little John" remove their identification factors. The Fool collects their quarterstaffs, and starts banging them together, then indicates that the rhythmic banging has given him an idea for a dance

Musicians pick up the beat. The Fool tumbles to the cart and finds six sticks. He throws them to the Morris Dancers, and organizes them into the right position. The villagers clap in rhythm till all is ready. Then the Morris Dancers dance an energetic stick dance. (For details of suggested dance routine, see Appendix)

Music 8: Stick Dance

During the stick dance, which is watched by all the others, any necessary preparations are made for the next sequence

The villagers applaud the stick dance, then go about selling their wares; their voices rise above the general hubbub, developing into a musical montage of tradesmen's cries

Music 9: Wild Flowers

Tessa ⎫ (*singing*)	
Elizabeth ⎭	
(*or children*)	Wild flowers!
	Wild flowers!
Jan ⎫	Fresh milk and warm,
Dorcas ⎭	Straight from the cow!
Pedlars	I've got ribbons and pins
(*2 men*)	And bright shiny buttons,
	And sugar and gingerbread!
Three Men	We have got good ale, boys
	Oh we have got good ale!
Butcher	I've got beef and venison!

The villager who is the butcher subsequently becomes the "Butcher" in the next Robin Hood story

All	May games, May games,

> Ev'rything for your May games!
> May games, May games,
> Ev'rything for your May Games!

This leads to a complicated counterpoint section, in which all the cries are sung on top of one another. Finally . . .

Butcher   I've got beef and venison!

He realizes he is singing on his own, and looks embarrassed. The others wander off leaving him alone, C

> I've got beef and venison!

He is rescued by George, who comes forward playing his lute/guitar

The Lights change to focus on George, and the Butcher, who features in the next story—"Robin Hood and the Butcher"

Everyone else becomes an audience again, until required in the story

Music 10: Allen-a-Dale's Link Song

George   We'll tell you a tale of this butcher so bold
(singing)   On his way to the market one morning
                     As he walked through the wood
                     In a flash, Robin Hood
                     Jumped on him without any warning.

"Robin Hood" appears from the shadows and grabs the "Butcher", who takes out his knife, threateningly. They grapple, but eventually "Robin Hood" proves himself the stronger, disarms the "Butcher" and pinions him from behind, an arm round his neck

"Robin Hood"   Not so fast master butcher, if you value your life,
                     I'm not one of your herd to be stuck with a knife.

                     Where are you going?
"Butcher"   To Market in Nottingham.
"Robin Hood"   Open your bags and let's see what you've got in 'em.

A Narrator takes up the tale

Narrator   When he saw all the meat, Robin had an idea.
                     He said,
"Robin Hood"   Master butcher, you've nothing to fear;

                     Your meat and your cart, your apron and hat—
                     I'll pay a fair price if you sell me all that.

Narrator   The price was agreed and a bargain was struck;
                     The butcher could hardly believe his good luck.

The "Butcher" departs happily

                     And Robin's eyes twinkled as they said their goodbyes,

"Robin Hood" (*to the audience*) The Sheriff is going to get a surprise.

	For it's said that he's put a price on my head,
	But I fancy that he'll pay the price instead.
Narrator	So he trundled the cart to Nottingham Market,
	And found by the castle a good place to park it.

"Robin Hood" mimes his journey. Another "Trader" sets up his stall nearby. "Shoppers" suggest a market

	He wasn't the only meat butcher around
"Trader"	Come buy my fresh venison, fivepence a pound.

The "Shoppers" crowd round him. "Robin Hood" sets up his stall

"Robin Hood"	He's cheating you rotten, fair ladies and gents.
	Come buy *my* fresh venison, a pound for *four* pence.

The "Shoppers" transfer their custom to "Robin Hood"

"Trader"	Now don't wander off, folks, just listen to me,
	Today's special offer, five pence down to three.

The "Shoppers" Ooh and Aah with pleasure and return to the "Trader"

"Robin Hood"	Wait! My cut price cuts are cheaper than any,
	Come buy my fresh venison, a pound for one penny.

The "Shoppers" return to "Robin Hood". The "Trader" shrugs and departs

	Those fly-by-night traders, you never can trust 'em.
	Two pounds for you, madam? Thanks for your custom.
Narrator	News of the bargain spread fast through the town.
	From the castle, the wife of the Sheriff came down.

Fanfare as the "Sheriff's Wife" greedily enters and barges her way through the "Shoppers"

"Sheriff's Wife"	Butcher, this venison, how much have you got?
"Robin Hood"	I've thirteen pounds left, lady.
"Sheriff's Wife"	I'll take the lot.

	But it looks such a weight.
Narrator	Smiled Robin,
"Robin Hood"	No trouble;
	Delivery's free, I'll be up at the double.

Pleased, the "Sheriff's Wife" leads "Robin Hood" to an area representing the castle

Narrator	Robin's plan was succeeding; he carried the parcel
	All the way up to and into the castle.

After miming his journey, "Robin Hood" hands the meat to the "Sheriff's Wife"

"Sheriff's Wife" (*aside*) This butcher, if pampered, I firmly conclude will

Be fearfully good for the size of my food bill.
(to "Robin Hood") Good Butcher, don't go, have a goblet of wine?
And do us the honour of staying to dine.

Narrator   Said Robin Hood,

"Robin Hood"   Thanks!

Narrator   And thus found himself able
To sit with his enemy, the Sheriff, at table.

The "Sheriff" enters

"Sheriff"   Come in!

Narrator   Leered the Sheriff.

"Sheriff"   Pray do take your place.

"Robin Hood"   I'll take,

Narrator   thought bold Robin

"Robin Hood"   that smile off your face!

They sit at a table to dine. A "Servant" brings wine and food

Narrator   With flattering words his praises he sung,
Till the wine started loos'ning the Sheriff's tongue.

He told tales of corruption, of cheating and guile,
Of men he'd imprisoned without any trial.

Of rigging and fixing, of bribing the jury;
Robin heartily laughed, thus disguising his fury.

"Sheriff"   What a splendid repast, your meat was delicious.
But where did it come from?

Narrator   He was getting suspicious.

"Sheriff"   Did you filch it?

Narrator   Cried Robin,

"Robin Hood"   No, don't be absurd.
For years I've been breeding my own special herd.

My beasts are the finest from Lincoln to York.

"Sheriff"   You're lying, good butcher, you're all wind and talk.

"Robin Hood"   Come and see for yourself, that I don't overrate them.

"Sheriff"   I *will* come and see them, *(aside)* and then confiscate
them!

He beckons two "Attendants" to follow him

Narrator   So after their meal without any delay
Deep into the forest they wended their way.

Music. "Robin Hood", "Sheriff", plus two "Attendants" set off. Others act trees or obstacles to suggest the forest. The lighting turns sinister

Through thicket and bramble, through stream and
through ditch,
The Sheriff grew weary and started to twitch.

"Sheriff"	This isn't a trick?
"Robin Hood"	Sir, I give you my word,
	Another few miles and you'll gaze on my herd.

"Robin Hood" suddenly blows his horn

	You can trust me, Sir,
Narrator	But the Sheriff cried,
"Sheriff"	But here in the forest the outlaws hide!

During the next two verses, unseen by the "Sheriff", his two "Attendants" are grabbed and carried off by "Robin Hood's men"

They're vicious and ruthless, they're up to no good;
And the worst of them all calls himself Robin Hood.

He's escaped me so far, like a wriggly worm,
But if I ever set eyes on him, I'll make him squirm.

"Robin Hood"	Pray calm yourself, sir, you'll frighten the deer,
	Look in that clearing and soon they'll appear.

Music as the "Deer" (villagers with antlers on their heads) enter and move around behind the trees or bushes, with only their antlers visible. (In the first London production, stools used in the Sheriff scene were picked up by the girls, who held them upside down over their heads to suggest antlers.) An eerie atmosphere

	I kept my word, sir. Admit they're fine.
"Sheriff"	They are, good butcher, what is more they are *mine*.

The "Sheriff" pulls a knife on "Robin Hood". Drums for tension. "Robin Hood" pretends to be afraid

"Robin Hood"	I don't understand, sir.
"Sheriff"	Now don't be alarmed.
	Just do as you're told and I'll see you're not harmed.
"Robin Hood"	How kind! But, sir, I don't need your protection;
	For me these deer have a special affection.

They're faithful and loyal and honest and true
You may fancy them, but they don't fancy you!

Percussion noises begin as the antlered villagers reveal themselves as "Outlaws", and start approaching the "Sheriff" menacingly

Take them out of the wood, if you reckon you could,
But first you must reckon with—Robin Hood!

Music, as "Robin Hood" reveals himself. The "Sheriff", in his confusion, finds his knife wrenched from his hand

"Sheriff"	Y-y-you're Robin Hood? Get him!
	(Looking round, then realizing his "Men" are gone)
	Where are my men?
"Robin Hood"	In heaven—or hell! You'll not see them again.

> Come on, sir, I'm waiting—I'm your wriggly worm.
> Now you've set eyes on me, pray make me squirm.

"Robin Hood" advances. The "Sheriff" retreats

"Sheriff"   You'll pay for this, Hood, you'll hang by your toes!
"Robin Hood"   On no, sir, *you'll* pay, you'll pay through the nose.

Music, as the antlered villagers approach and surround the "Sheriff"

"Sheriff"   Mercy, I beg you, sir, please spare my life,
                   For the sake of my children, for the sake of my wife.

"Robin Hood"   But what of the price you put on my head?
(*to the others*) Should I let him live, when he wished me dead?

The others shake their heads or cry "no"

"Sheriff"   I swear by our Lady, if you set me free
                   Your safety in Sherwood, will I guarantee.

Pause

"Robin Hood"   Very well, sir, I b'lieve you, but b'lieve me you'll find
                   That if there's a next time we won't be so kind.

George comes forward

George (*speaking*) The Sheriff had made them a promise
                   So the outlaws escorted him back
                   And so he couldn't retrace
                   His steps to this place
                   They covered his head with a sack.

As the girls cover the "Sheriff's" head with a sack, the "Outlaws" take his money and valuables

Then the music strikes up for a traditional Horn Dance, in which the antlered villagers "attack" each other like stags. A suggested routine for this dance is to be found in the Appendix

Music 11: Horn Dance

The others clap in accompaniment, jubilant at the victory over the "Sheriff". Then the Lights change back to the May Games state, as all start singing at the blindfolded "Sheriff"

Music 12: Take the Scorn

All   Take the scorn to wear the horn,
  (*singing*)   It was the crest when you were born.
                   Your father's father wore it
                   And your father wore it too.

Having sung their meaningful diatribe against the "Sheriff", the atmosphere changes as they all happily dance around him. The lighting brightens, to suggest a warm midday

Music 12a: Hal-an-tow

Hal-an-tow
Jolly rumbelow,
We were up
Long before the day-o!
To welcome in the summer,
The summer and the May-o!
For summer is a-coming in
And winter's gone away-o!

Dance. (For suggested routine, see the Appendix.) Then a final chorus, during which the company escort the blindfolded "Sheriff" away, and eventually out of the auditorium

Hal-an-tow
Jolly rumbelow,
We were up
Long before the day-o!
To welcome in the summer,
The summer and the May-o!
For summer is a-coming in
And winter's gone away-o!

Extra chorus if necessary. Silence. The company has gone

ACT II

The same

The lighting bursts up as the company return singing and drumming. It is still midday

Music 13: Hal-an-tow (Reprise)

All Hal-an-tow
(*singing*) Jolly rumbelow,
We were up
Long before the day-o!
To welcome in the summer
The summer and the May-o!
For summer is a-coming in
And winter's gone away-o!

Hal-an-tow
Jolly rumbelow,
We were up
Long before the day-o!
To welcome in the summer
The summer and the May-o!
For summer is a-coming in
And winter's gone away-o!

As the song progresses, the company set up the stage as Nottingham Fair. Music continues, as fairground activity begins. The company demonstrate a number of sporting pastimes. The milkmaids—Jan and Dorcas—do a step dance. Two men wrestle. Two men join battle in singlestick. Any other skills of the company, such as juggling, acrobatics or fire-eating could also be employed here. The sequence could be interspersed with, and certainly closes with, a final chorus

Hal-an-tow
Jolly rumbelow,
We were up
Long before the day-o!
To welcome in the summer
The summer and the May-o!
For summer is a-coming in
And winter's gone away-o!

Robin Hood and Little John
Have both gone to the fair-o
So we will leave the merry greenwood
And see what they did there-o.

All cheer and applaud as George comes forward playing his lute/guitar. The lighting changes to take us into the story of "Robin Hood and Sir Guy of Gisborne"

Music 14: Allen-a-Dale's Link Song

George   We'll tell you how Robin and his Merry Men
(*singing*)   Made a visit to Nottingham Fair.

"Robin Hood", "Little John" and other "Outlaws" enter the scene

They thought it was wise
To go in disguise
So no-one would know they were there.

Fanfare. The "Sheriff", presiding over the fair, stands and the crowd is silent

"Sheriff"   Citizens all, the time has come
(*speaking*)   For the archery competition.

Applause. The target is brought out

This silver arrow will be the prize
For the man with the most precision.

"Robin Hood" (*aside to "Little John"*) I think we ought to enter this
There's no-one here could match us.
"Little John"   But if the Sheriff should suspect
He's bound to try to snatch us.

For after our last escapade
He's bound to bear a grudge.
"Sheriff"   My guest, Sir Guy of Gisborne,
I invite to be the judge.

Murmurings of discontent in the crowd as "Sir Guy" is presented. Jan takes over the narration

Jan   Sir Guy was a blackhearted villain
Well known for his wheeling and dealing.
Where corruption was high in high places
Sir Guy would be up on the ceiling.

Said he,
"Sir Guy"   The target is ready.
Let the competition start!
Jan   Said Robin,
"Robin Hood"   I would the target
Were Guy of Gisborne's heart.

"Robin Hood" and "Little John" put their hoods up, to avoid their faces being recognized. Fanfare for the start of the competition. Music and sound effects as the company mime the archery competition. "Archers" take aim and shoot at the target. "Sir Guy" calls their score. The arrows whistle. The crowd applaud or boo

Jan   So now the archers took their turn;
                                 From long bows taut the arrows flew,
                                 Splitting the target with a thud—
                                 The average score—red, black or
"Sir Guy" (*calling the score*)   Blue!

Applause

                                 Next!
Jan   Little John now took his aim . . .

Tension, drum roll. "Little John" fires

"Sir Guy"   A gold!
"Sheriff"   Well shot!
"Robin Hood"   Good try!
Jan   Robin Hood was last to shoot . . .

Tension, drum roll. "Robin Hood" fires. Gasp from the crowd

"Sheriff"   Good Lord!
"Sir Guy"   He wins, he hit the eye!

Applause. The "Sheriff" gets ready to present the arrow. Fanfare. "Robin Hood", head still covered, goes to collect the prize

"Sheriff"   Congratulations, sir, what skill!
                      Please tell us if you would
                      Your name, and let us see your face.

"Robin Hood" shows his face

                      Aaah! Saints preserve us!—Robin Hood!

"Robin Hood" blows his horn. His "men" all reveal themselves. Exciting dramatic music as a fight breaks out, involving as many people as possible as "Robin Hood's Men" and the "Sheriff's Men". As much variety of fighting as possible should be employed—handfighting, swordfighting, quarterstaff fighting, slapstick perhaps

Gradually the combatants become exhausted or are slain, leaving two areas of fighting—(1) "Robin Hood" and "Guy of Gisborne" (2) "Little John" taking on several of the "Sheriff's Men". The two areas are isolated in separate pools of light. It is suggested that as the action cuts from one area to the other, the lights dim or brighten accordingly

"Robin Hood" and "Sir Guy" are seen in unarmed combat. "Little John" is caught by the "Sheriff's Men", and held struggling. "Sir Guy" produces a dagger, but after a short struggle "Robin Hood" quickly overpowers "Sir

Guy". However, "Sir Guy" manages to get out his horn. He is about to blow it

"Sir Guy" (*calling*) Help me, Sir Sheriff!

"Robin Hood"   Oh no, Sir Guy, you're on your own,
                        The Sheriff's men don't hear you.
                        You've had your fun—it's one to one.

"Sir Guy"   Let's fight then, I don't fear you.

Tense drumming as "Robin Hood" and "Sir Guy" have a dramatic fight. First they use daggers. In the struggle, "Sir Guy" drops his dagger. "Robin Hood" chivalrously throws away his too. They wrestle. The fight veers from side to side. Finally "Robin Hood" wins—leaving "Sir Guy" unconscious. Other "Outlaws" rush in

Will Scarlett (*breathless*) Robin, quickly, Little John
                        The Sheriff's men have got him!

Jan   Robin worked out what to do . . .

"Robin Hood" suddenly takes "Sir Guy's" horn and blows it

"Robin Hood" (*having an idea*) The jacket!

The "Outlaws" help "Robin Hood" change coats with "Sir Guy"

                                      Right, now bind and knot him.

The "Outlaws" do so, then support him (because he is still unconscious), with his back view visible. "Robin Hood" covers his face with "Sir Guy's" Hood

Jan   The Sheriff heard the horn.

The "Sheriff" enters from his area, accompanied by two of his "Men" leading the tied-up "Little John"

"Sheriff" (*calling*)   Sir Guy!
                        Is everything all right?

"Robin Hood" (*impersonating "Sir Guy's" voice*)
                        Indeed it is, sir. Robin Hood
                        Has fought his final fight.

"Sheriff"   At last, at last. Well done, Sir Guy!

He kicks the rear of the man he thinks is "Robin Hood" (in fact, "Sir Guy")

                        Take that, and that you wretch;
                      You'll pay for all your villainy
                      You're off to meet Jack Ketch.

"Robin Hood" (*indicating "Little John"*)
                      But who's *this* man, Sir Sheriff?

"Sheriff"   Another of the band.

"Robin Hood"   If you will grant permission, sir,
                      He'll perish by my hand.

Jan   The Sheriff saw no reason
                      Not to give "Sir Guy" the nod.

"Sheriff"   With all my blessings, he's your prize.

"Robin Hood" picks up a dagger and advances on "Little John". Tension music

"Robin Hood"   Prepare to meet your God.

"Robin Hood" suddenly cuts "Little John" free and reveals himself to the "Sheriff". Fanfare

                  The tables turn once more sir.

The "Sheriff" sees what has happened and gasps with astonishment and fear

                  What's up? I see you frown!
                  Now Little John, take off your prize!

* "Little John" picks up the "Sheriff" and carries him off screaming*

"Sheriff"   Get off me! Put me down!

Drums for tension, as "Robin Hood" turns to "Sir Guy"

"Robin Hood"   You, sir,
Jan   said Robin quietly,
                  Approaching false Sir Guy—
"Robin Hood"   The laws of honest outlaws
                  Now sentence you to die.

Music, as the Lighting changes dramatically, sinister drumming begins and leads into a very sinister dance

Music 15: Sword Dance

It is basically a sword dance, with "Sir Guy" (who has put on a false head) being surrounded by "Outlaws" who gradually place their swords around his neck. (For suggested dance routine, see appendix) The dance reaches a dramatic climax as everybody yells. The swords are closed around "Guy of Gisborne's" neck, then suddenly withdrawn; his head falls off. Black-out

After a pause, through the darkness we hear a humming dirge, which creates a religious atmosphere for the next Robin Hood story

Music 16: This Ae Night

Voices   This ae night
  (singing)   This ae night
                  Ev'ry night and all
                  Fire and salt and candlelight
                  And Christ receive thy soul.

During the chant, the Lights come up as the "Bishop" enters on horseback (the Hobby Horse), with swollen saddlebags. Behind him process the "Abbess" and "Two Monks". As they proceed through the auditorium, the chanting continues, leading us into the story of "Robin Hood and the Bishop"

> If thou from here away do pass
> Ev'ry night and all
> To Whinny Moor thou com'st at last
> And Christ receive thy soul.

Repeat first verse—"This Ae Night"—if necessary

Suddenly the chanting is interrupted as two "Outlaws" emerge, bows and arrows poised

"Outlaws"	Stop where you are, Lord Bishop.
"Monks"	God save us!
"Abbess"	Aaaaaah!
"Bishop"	Keep calm!
(to the "Outlaws")	How dare you hold up holy folk And interrupt our psalm.
"Outlaws"	Just cut the cackle, Bishop.
"Bishop"	You'll pay for this, you'll see.
"Outlaws"	Now kindly climb down from your horse Before we count to three.
"Bishop"	I've never heard such nonsense.
"Outlaws"	One!
"Bishop"	May you rot in Hell!
"Outlaws"	Two!
"Bishop'	I'll not dismount for you.
"Outlaws" *(taking aim)*	Three!
"Bishop"	Oh, very well!

As the "Bishop" dismounts, "Friar Tuck" enters

"Friar Tuck"	Just what is going on here? I pray you hold your fire. You can't waylay a bishop!
"Bishop"	God bless you, holy Friar.
"Friar Tuck" *(angry)*	You ought to be ashamed, lads.
"Outlaws"	Forgive us, we repent!
"Friar Tuck"	Putting the wind up holy folk.
"Outlaws"	We'll give it up for Lent.
"Bishop"	I absolve your sins, my sons
"Outlaws"	Oh bless your lordship, thank you.
"Friar Tuck"	You don't deserve it, damn your eyes; I've got a mind to spank you!
(Getting angrier)	God's chosen blessed pilgrims How dare you treat them thus?
"Bishop"	Good Friar, pray be silent You're making too much fuss.

"Friar Tuck's" anger gradually becomes thinly veiled irony, which makes the "Bishop" and the "Holy Party" uncomfortable

"Friar Tuck"   I'm sorry, but these rogues must know
                        How grave is their offence.
                        To rob these landlords—
"Bishop"   Landlords?
"Friar Tuck"   Returning with their rents.

The "Holy Party" look nervously at each other

                        Weighed down with all the money
                        They've squeezed from their poor tenants
                        Who starve and strain to keep alive
                        And lead a life of penance.

                        You wretched outlaws rob the rich
                        To help your poorer brother.
                        These upright, godly clerics rob
                        The *poor*—to help each other.

                        An outlaw or a bishop—
                        Now who's the greater sinner?
"Bishop"   I think we'd best be on our way
                        Or we'll be late for dinner.

                        Goodbye, good Friar, and thank you
                        For coming to our aid.
"Friar Tuck"   I saved your lives.
"Bishop"   God bless you.
"Friar Tuck"   Now I must be repaid.

"Bishop"   The blessing of a bishop
                        Is surely rich reward.
"Friar Tuck"   I fancy something richer.
"Bishop"   That's all I can afford.

                        The blessing of a bishop's
                        I repeat, reward enough.
"Friar Tuck"   But I was really thinking
                        Of more material stuff!

The "Bishop" makes a swift move to go. The "Outlaws" take aim

                        Stop where you are, Lord Bishop.
"Monks"   God save us!
"Abbess"   Aaaaaah!
"Bishop"   Keep calm!
"Friar Tuck"   Hand over all your money
                        And you'll not come to harm.

"Bishop"   You're not a friar at all!
                        You're an outlaw of the wood.
"Friar Tuck"   I *am* a friar—I'm chaplain
                        To the men of Robin Hood.

Other "Outlaws" emerge and surround the "Holy Party"

"Bishop"	Robin Hood your master?
"Monks"	God save us!
"Abbess"	Aaaaah!
"Bishop" (*irritated*)	Be quiet!
	A man of God in league with Hood?
"Friar Tuck"	I proudly don't deny it.

He has no time for bishops,
Their avarice, their greed.
He'll give your unearned income
To men of greater need.

So come on—hand it over,
Your money, ev'ry penny.

"Bishop"	But, foolish Friar, I cannot.
	You see, I haven't any.
"Friar Tuck"	You haven't?
"Bishop"	No, I haven't.
"Monks" **"Abbess"** }	We've not a groat between us!
"Bishop"	So, I'm afraid, fat Friar,
	You can't take us to the cleaners!
"Friar Tuck"	God moves, they say, mysteriously—
	His mercy will provide;
	For sure a bishop's solemn prayer
	Could never be denied.

So on your knees and quickly,
Make contact with your maker.
And if he doesn't heed our need
You'll need an undertaker.

The "Bishop", "Monks" and "Abbess" fall to their knees, and sing their prayer in harmony

Music 16a: O Heavenly Father

"Bishop" **"Monks"** **"Abbess"** }	O heavenly Father, hear us We're in a spot of trouble If we don't get some money It won't be very funny, Please send some at the double. Amen.

Music as the "Outlaws" search the Hobby Horse, and the "Holy Party". Large sums of money are found in the saddlebags. The "Monks" and "Abbess" wail

"Friar Tuck" (*with mock joy*)	A miracle! A miracle!
	God heard your supplication!
	His blessed mercy saved you—

This calls for celebration!

Music. As the company excitedly cheer, the lighting changes to indicate early evening. We are back at the May Games

The "Holy Party", not having time to change costume, gets swept up in the revelries. This means that during the dance, the May Games villagers blend with the "Robin Hood" characters, for the first time

Music 17: Dance, Dance

All (*singing*)   Dance, dance, dance all day
                            Dance your cares away.
                            Pay the piper and call the tune
                            And dance with me today.

                            Today it is a special day
                            It is the first of May.
                            So pay the piper and call the tune
                            And dance with me today.

The music continues for a joyful dance in which the "Holy Party" are forced to participate. Then the Fool performs a tricky Bali-type stick dance, in which he is in severe danger of getting his ankles rapped if he doesn't avoid the clicking sticks. For details of the dance, see Appendix. After a while, the Fool invites the "Bishop" to have a go. He declines, but is forced to. Reluctantly the "Bishop" starts to dance, and has to really jump hard and vigorously to avoid being hurt. Eventually, however, the "Bishop" begins to enjoy himself, and the whole "Holy Party" clap and join in with the spirit. Finally the whole company sing the chorus

                            Dance, dance, dance all day
                            Dance your cares away.
                            Pay the piper and call the tune
                            And dance with me today.

The May Games folk congratulate the "Bishop" on his dancing. The "Bishop" begins to remove his vestments. The lighting subtly changes to suggest sunset. Warm, orange shades

Dickran Hang on. Don't take 'em off. You've got some more "bishoping" to do. Look, it's nearly sunset.

Elizabeth (*very serious*) And we haven't chosen our May Queen yet.

"Friar Tuck" stands forward

"Friar Tuck"   Peter, our King of the Day
                        Who will you take for your Queen of the May?

Peter looks around

Peter I choose ... Jan!

All voice their agreement

Jan (*taking the ash-leaf from her pocket*) The ash leaf was right!

"Friar Tuck" We need attendants. Who will attend on the King and the Queen?

Hands shoot up

(*Choosing*) Tessa. And Dickran.

Cheers. Tessa triumphantly waves her ash-leaf at the other girls. Tessa and Dickram find two green boughs, and with them make an archway for Jan

"Friar Tuck" steps forward and sings an introduction to the story of "Robin Hood and Allen-a-Dale". The lighting changes

Music 18: Before the Maid Weds

"Friar Tuck" (*singing*)	But before the maid weds with the King of the May There's time for just one more tale. And as loving's in season Then that's a good reason For singing of Allen-a-Dale.
All	Allen, Allen-a-Dale, For singing of Allen-a-Dale.

The story is sung by the company, in unison, or split up into solo lines as required. "Friar Tuck", however, should start and finish it. The "Robin Hood" characters mime the story

"Friar Tuck" (*singing*)	For young Allen the minstrel was handsome and bold With the ladies he just couldn't fail. And many's the maid That has knelt down and prayed For the love of young Allen-a-Dale.
Chorus	Allen, Allen-a-Dale, For the love of young Allen-a-Dale.
Company	There was one pretty maid who was fairer than spring And Allen was oft by her side. The first time he saw her Allen fell down before her And said,
"Allen-a-Dale"	Pretty maid be my bride.
Chorus	Allen, Allen-a-Dale, He said, "Pretty maid be my bride."
Company	Now if she'd said yes, then as you might guess They'd have wed in the church down the lane; But though he had pricked them Sly Cupid had tricked them, And the maid sadly sang this refrain.
"Pretty Maid"	Allen, Allen-a-Dale,
Chorus	And the maid sadly sang this refrain.

"Pretty Maid"	An old man came courting me, Hey ding doorum, An old man came courting me Me being young. An old man came courting me, Fain he would marry me
Chorus	Maids when you're young never wed an old man.
"Pretty Maid"	My parents they promised me, Hey ding doorum, My parents they promised me Me being young, My parents they promised me This old man's bride to be,
Chorus	Maids when you're young Never wed an old man.
Company	Now Robin was passing and heard this sad tale And determined to put matters right. So plans they were laid To save the young maid From the arms of this toothless old knight.
	So Robin, disguised as a minstrel, set off For the wedding the following day. And Allen and John Well, they both followed on Just to see that the maid got fair play.
	Now the Bishop was partial to tunes on the harp And he asked in a manner imperious;
"Bishop"	Come, Minstrel, an air, For this happy young pair,
Company **"Robin Hood"**	To which Robin replied: You're not serious.
Company	Enough of this nonsense, Then Robin declared And he threw off his cloak there and then Robin Hood! came a shout And the old man passed out And the Bishop, in fear, cried,
"Bishop"	Amen.
Company	Then John read the banns for young Allen-a- Dale, And the Bishop, who valued his life With a sword to his head He declared them
"Bishop"	Well wed
"Friar Tuck"	And the couple became man and wife.

Chorus   Allen, Allen-a-Dale
                                    And the couple became man and wife.

All sing a wedding hymn to the happy couple

Music 19: Wedding Hymn

All   Come write me down, ye powers above,
                                    The man that first created love.
                                    For I've a diamond in my eye
                                    Where all my joys and comforts lie
                                    Where all my joys and comforts lie.

*A short musical bridge as everyone crowds in to congratulate "Allen-a-Dale"
and "Pretty Maid", who excitedly holds up her ash-leaf. The "Bishop" stands
behind them, giving them his enforced blessing. The crowd carry boughs to
screen the married couple, and mask them completely*

                                    So in the church the very next day
                                    They were married by asking as I've heard say
                                    So now that girl she is his wife,
                                    She will prove his comfort day and night,
                                    She will prove his comfort day and night.

*The crowd back away, revealing the fact that in place of "Pretty Maid" and
"Allen-a-Dale", now stand Jan and Peter. "Friar Tuck" has taken over from
the "Bishop"*

*The lighting changes and we are back at the May Games, all except "Friar
Tuck" who remains in his Robin Hood character to perform the ritual
marriage. Shafts of light hit the couple and the company hum the melody as the
preparations for the ritual marriage take place. The girls take Jan aside and
prepare her for the wedding, giving her garlands of flowers and putting blossom
in her hair. The men take Peter to the other side and dress him up in cloak,
crown and greenery, sticking leaves or a green mask on his face. Ceremonially
the couple come together under the maypole, and, directed by "Friar Tuck"
join hands. The lighting changes as shafts of light help to suggest the fact that
the marriage symbolizes the arrival of summer, fertility, new growth, etc.*

"Friar Tuck"   Now is the time for the Queen of the May
  (*speaking*)   To be joined in hand with the Lord of the Day.

He joins their hands. The pose is held for a short time, then music breaks out

Music 20: Dance, Dance (*Reprise*) *followed by*
Music 21: Circle Dance (*Reprise*)

*The company dance jubilantly round the maypole and round Peter and Jan,
who remain c*

All   Dance, dance, dance all day
  (*singing*)   Dance your cares away.
                                    Pay the piper and call the tune
                                    And dance with me today.

> Dance, dance, dance all day
> Dance your cares away.
> Pay the piper and call the tune
> And dance with me today.

All stop dancing and face the audience

(*In unison*)   We've welcomed in the first of May
                                 Our King and Queen we've crowned.
                                 We've paid the piper and called the tune
                                 We've danced our final round.

The company hold out their ribbons, enclosing within them Peter and Jan, the King and Queen of the May. The music stops

In silence, Jan fetches a bow and ceremonially hands it to Peter, then exits. Peter becomes "Robin Hood" once more and now performs the final ritual of May Day. He mimes taking a high aim with his long bow. As he does so, the others pull taut their ribbons. "Robin Hood" fires an imaginary arrow, as though towards the sun. Optional sound effect as the arrow whistles through the air. The others release their ribbons

Black-out. Silence

CURTAIN

FURNITURE AND PROPERTY LIST

PROLOGUE

On stage: nil
No props required

ACT I

On stage: nil
In addition to the props listed below, each Robin Hood character should have an identification factor for use in the Robin Hood playlets—see Author's Introduction on page vii.

Props required: Drawstring purse with ash-leaves **(Jan)**
    Leafy branch **(Dickran)**
    Leafy branch **(Philip)**
    Decorated hoops **(Dorcas, Jan, Children)**
    Lute/guitar **(George)**
    Decorated cart containing greenery and materials for beer bower; identification factors for Robin Hood characters; 6 sticks **(Alan, Ross** and **Jan)**
    Jack-in-the-Green garland **(Peter)**
    False nose **(Comic Friar)**
    Bladder on a stick **(Fool)**
    Maypole with ribbons **(Boy, Fool** and others**)**
    Tables and benches **(Villagers)**
    Trays of mugs of ale **(Tessa** and **Elizabeth)**
    4 trick glasses of ale **(Tessa)**
    Ribbons for stream effect **(Company)**
    Bag containing pie; sword, horn **("Robin Hood")**
    Bucklers **("Friar Tuck")**
    Dog masks **(Villagers)**
    Food and drink **(Villagers)**
    Bells, handkerchiefs **(Morris Dancers)**
    2 quarterstaffs **(Narrator)**
    Horn **("Robin Hood")**
    Tradespeople's wares—flowers, milk etc. **(Villagers)**
    Apron, hat, knife, cart of meat **("Butcher")**
    Meat stall **("Trader")**
    Knife, money, valuables **("Sheriff")**
    Wine and food **("Servant")**
    Antlers **("Outlaws")**
    Sack **("Outlaws")**

ACT II

Props required: Materials for Nottingham Fair including target, silver arrow **(Company)**

Lute/guitar **(George)**

Weapons—swords, quarterstaffs etc. **("Outlaws", "Sheriff's Men")**

Dagger, horn **("Sir Guy")**

Dagger, horn **("Robin Hood")**

Rope **("Sheriff's Men")**

Rope **("Outlaws")**

False head **("Sir Guy")**

Saddlebags containing money **("Bishop")**

Bows and arrows **("Outlaws")**

Sticks for dance **(Fool)**

Ash-leaf **(Jan)**

Ash-leaf **(Tessa)**

Green boughs **(Tessa** and **Dikran)**

Ash-leaf **("Pretty Maid")**

Green boughs **(Company)**

Garlands of flowers (for **Jan)**

Cloak, crown, greenery, mask **(for Peter)**

Bow **(Jan)**

LIGHTING PLOT

Practical fittings required: nil
An open space. Various simple settings

Prologue

To open: House Lights up
Cue 1   When ready   (Page 1)
           Fade House Lights; bring up general lighting on playing area

Cue 2   **Michael:** "Share them with us. Everyone."   (Page 1)
           Fade to Black-out

ACT I

To open: Black-out

Cue 3   Clock chimes 3 o'clock   (Page 3)
           Slowly fade up shafts of moonlight

Cue 4   Clock chimes 4 o'clock   (Page 3)
           Increase moonlight

Cue 5   **Jan:** "Peter is the one for me!"   (Page 4)
           Fade lights

Cue 6   As **Dikran** sings   (Page 4)
           Increase lighting as dawn rises—continue to increase during song

Cue 7   **Jack-in-the-Green** stands up in the cart   (Page 5)
           Green spot on **Jack-in-the-Green**

Cue 8   **Jan** moves forward to **Peter**   (Page 6)
           Change to white spot on **Peter** *and* **Jan**

Cue 9   Garland is hoisted up maypole   (Page 6)
           Increase lighting

Cue 10   **Peter** walks to front, his arms raised   (Page 6)
           Shafts of light on **Peter** *from above, below and behind*

Cue 11   As **Tessa** and **Elizabeth** bring in trays of ale   (Page 7)
           Change to general lighting

Cue 12   **George** starts playing introduction to **Music 4** (Page 7)
           Change to Robin Hood lighting

Cue 13   At end of **Music 4**—**Comic Friar** left C   (Page 9)
           Change to May Games lighting

Cue 14   **Dikran** begins to tell story of Robin Hood and Friar Tuck   (Page 10)
           Change to Robin Hood lighting

Cue 15   **"Friar Tuck":** "Where d'you keep your venison?"   (Page 14)
              Change to May Games lighting—bright sunshine

Cue 16   **George:** "No! Stay there."   (Page 16)
              Change to Robin Hood lighting

Cue 17   Fight reaches crescendo: deadlock   (Page 17)
              Change lighting—optional strobe lighting

Cue 18   **"Robin Hood"** falls into "water"   (Page 18)
              Return to previous lighting

Cue 19   **"Robin Hood"** and **"Little John"** bow   (Page 19)
              Change to May Games lighting

Cue 20   **Butcher** stands alone C; **George** comes forward   (Page 20)
              Change to Robin Hood lighting

Cue 21   **Narrator:** ". . . they wended their way."   (Page 22)
              Change to sinister lighting

Cue 22   **"Deer"** appear   (Page 23)
              Fade lighting further—eerie atmosphere

Cue 23   At end of **Horn Dance**   (Page 24)
              Change to May Games lighting

Cue 24   **All** dance happily round **"Sheriff"**   (Page 24)
              Increase lighting to suggest warm midday

ACT II

To open: Black-out

Cue 25   When ready   (Page 26)
              Snap up lighting—warm, midday sunshine

Cue 26   All cheer and applaud as **George** comes forward playing lute/   (Page 27)
                guitar
              Change to Robin Hood lighting

Cue 27   As fighting comes down to two areas   (Page 28)
              Pool of light on **"Robin Hood"** *and* **"Sir Guy"**; *pool of light on*
                "Little John" *and* **"Sheriff's Men"**—*dim and brighten pools as
                action cuts from one area to other*

Cue 28   **"Robin Hood":** "Now sentence you to die."   (Page 30)
              Change to dramatic, sinister lighting

Cue 29   **"Sir Guy's"** head falls off   (Page 30)
              Black-out

Cue 30   During chant **"This Ae Night"**   (Page 30)
              Bring up Robin Hood lighting

Cue 31   **"Friar Tuck":** "This calls for celebration." *Company cheer*   (Page 33)
              Change lighting to early evening

Cue 32   As **Company** sing chorus   (Page 34)
              Change lighting to warm, glowing sunset

EFFECTS PLOT

PROLOGUE

No cues

ACT I

Cue 1	When ready *Echoing footsteps, followed by clock bell chiming 2 o'clock*	(Page 3)
Cue 2	**Voice 1:** "... may the good Lord keep ..." *Handbell rings*	(Page 3)
Cue 3	**Voice 2:** "... whilst you sleep." *Handbell rings; clock chimes 3 o'clock*	(Page 3)
Cue 4	**Voice 3:** "... and all's well." *Handbell rings*	(Page 3)
Cue 5	**Voice 4:** "... that rings the bell." *Handbell rings; clock chimes 4 o'clock*	(Page 3)
Cue 6	**Voice 5:** "... good-day to you ..." *Handbell rings*	(Page 3)
Cue 7	**Voice 6:** "... gather the magic dew." *Handbell rings*	(Page 3)
Cue 8	**All** (*with a shout*): "Little John!" *Fanfare*	(Page 19)
Cue 9	**"Sheriff's Wife"** enters *Fanfare*	(Page 21)

ACT II

Cue 10	**George** (*singing*): "... know they were there." *Fanfare*	(Page 27)
Cue 11	**"Robin Hood"** and **"Little John"** put up their hoods *Fanfare*	(Page 28)
Cue 12	During competition *Whistle and thud as arrows hit target*	(Page 28)
Cue 13	Applause; **"Sheriff"** gets ready to present arrow *Fanfare*	(Page 28)
Cue 14	**"Robin Hood"** reveals himself to **"Sheriff"** *Fanfare*	(Page 30)
Cue 15	(*optional*) **"Robin Hood"** fires imaginary arrow *Whistle of arrow*	(Page 38)

DANCE APPENDIX

The dances in this play can be performed in two ways:

(a) As theatrical impressions of traditional dances, which allows plenty of scope for any acrobatic or gymnastic skills that the cast may possess, or
(b) As authentic folk dances.

Either way they should not be treated as sacred fetishes. Ideally a combination of the two approaches would be nearer the original conception—that is, taking the elements of genuine traditional dances and turning them into a theatrical experience by the use of colourful costumes and exciting steps and acrobatics. And above all, plenty of *enthusiasm*.

The Morris Dance
Any traditional morris dance that fits the music or a made up stylized dance in which six handkerchief-waving, bell-jingling dancers form two lines and advance, retire, cross over, etc., with suitable vigour.

There are morris dance clubs in most parts of the country and if there is no choreographer or folk dancer in the company, we suggest contacting the nearest morris team for help and advice.

Stick Dance
Six dancers face each other in pairs, as in diagram (I):

(diagram I)

18–24″ sticks held in right hands. Sticks are clashed right and left on 1st and 3rd beats of the bar, with double clash to finish on 16th bar.

Then (1) passes right shoulder to (2) left shoulder to (3), etc., (2) and (3) follow, so everyone weaves in and out for 16 bars (diagram II).

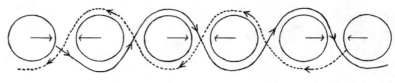

(diagram II)

The Horn Dance
This can be based on the traditional Horn Dance from Abbotts Bromley in Staffordshire or, like the other dances, it can be improvized by the company. The six dancers could work out a series of movements involving the two lines of deer-men advancing towards each other with horns lowered like stags fighting and then retiring, then perhaps advancing with the lines passing through each other right shoulder to right shoulder. This could then become a circle dance for eight or sixteen bars before turning to circle the other way, before forming up in two lines to start again.

The Sword Dance
This can be a genuine long-sword dance learnt from a local morris or sword-dance team or from Cecil Sharp's book *The Sword Dances of Northern England* (EP Publishing Ltd 1977) or it can be a choreographed theatrical version of a sword-dance using whatever figures you like. The only stipulations are that the dancers circle around the kneeling **"Sir Guy"** and finish with a "lock" of swords around his neck which, when sharply withdrawn, simulate a beheading.

In England "sword" dances are not danced with real swords as in Scotland, but with long flat pieces of wood or metal with a handle on one end. They should be about one metre long and three centimetres wide and half a centimetre thick. Wooden "swords" are available from the English Folk Dance and Song Society in London. The dancers could march around clockwise for eight bars, banging their swords on the floor inside their circle. Next, perhaps, eight bars anti-clockwise, clashing their swords in the air, forming a cone above **"Sir Guy's"** head. Then circle round in single file carrying swords in right hand laid over left shoulder, left hand holding the point of the sword in front. After eight or sixteen bars of music all stop and turn right into centre bringing own sword over head down to waist level. The swords should all now be locked into a six-pointed star (see diagram III) over **"Sir Guy's"** head. Push them well together and straighten up the sides of the "lock".

The leader or captain of the dancers then holds up the "lock" for the audience to see and all march around **"Sir Guy"**. After eight bars the "lock" is lowered over **"Sir Guy's"** head for another eight bars, each dancer holding a handle. At the conclusion of the music each dancer pulls his own sword free and **"Sir Guy's"** body falls to the floor on a black-out.

Quarterstaff Dance
Two poles are held, as shown in diagram (IV), and banged on the floor, then clashed together in rhythm. The dancer improvizes a series of steps, jumping in and out of the poles between the clashes; the clashes and steps get progressively faster and more complex as the dance goes on.

The poles could be quarter staffs or lighter bamboo rods or canes.

These are very basic ideas which can be embellished if required.

Any more information on morris, sword, stick and horn dances can be obtained from the English Folk Dance and Song Society, 2 Regents Park Road, London N2.

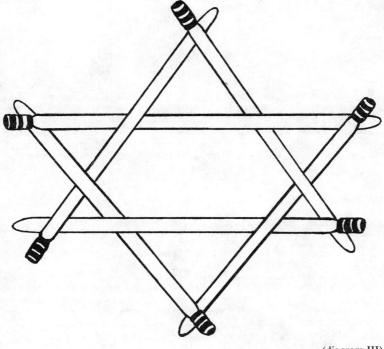

(diagram III)

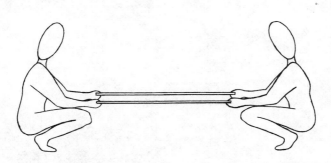

(diagram IV)